HAL•LEONARD®
SAXOPHONE PLAY-ALONG

AUDIO
ACCESS
INCLUDED

PLAYBACK+
Speed • Pitch • Balance • Loop

SMOOTH Jazz

VOL. 12

PARTS FOR SAXOPHONES

Play 8 Songs with Notation and Sound-alike Audio

To access audio visit:
www.halleonard.com/mylibrary

Enter Code
5398-0162-3658-2511

Musicians:
Saxophone – Jason Weber
Guitar – Mike DeRose
Drums & Percussion – Jack Dune
Bass – Chris Kringel
Keyboard – Brian Myers & Lou Cucunato
Trumpet – Matt Antoniewicz

Produced by Chris Kringel

ISBN 978-1-5400-0407-9

7777 W. BLUEMOUND RD. P.O.BOX 13819 MILWAUKEE, WI 53213

Visit Hal Leonard Online at
www.halleonard.com

CONTENTS

Bermuda Nights

By Gerald Albright

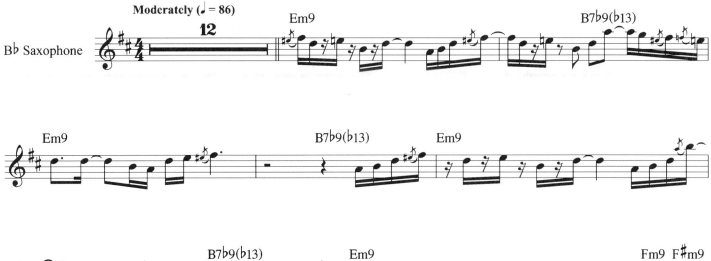

Blue Water

By Brian Culbertson and Eric Marienthal

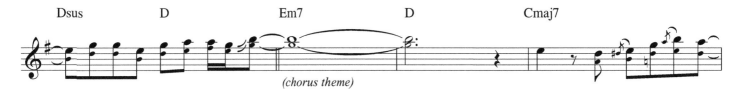

(chorus theme)

(chorus theme continues)

(chorus theme continues)

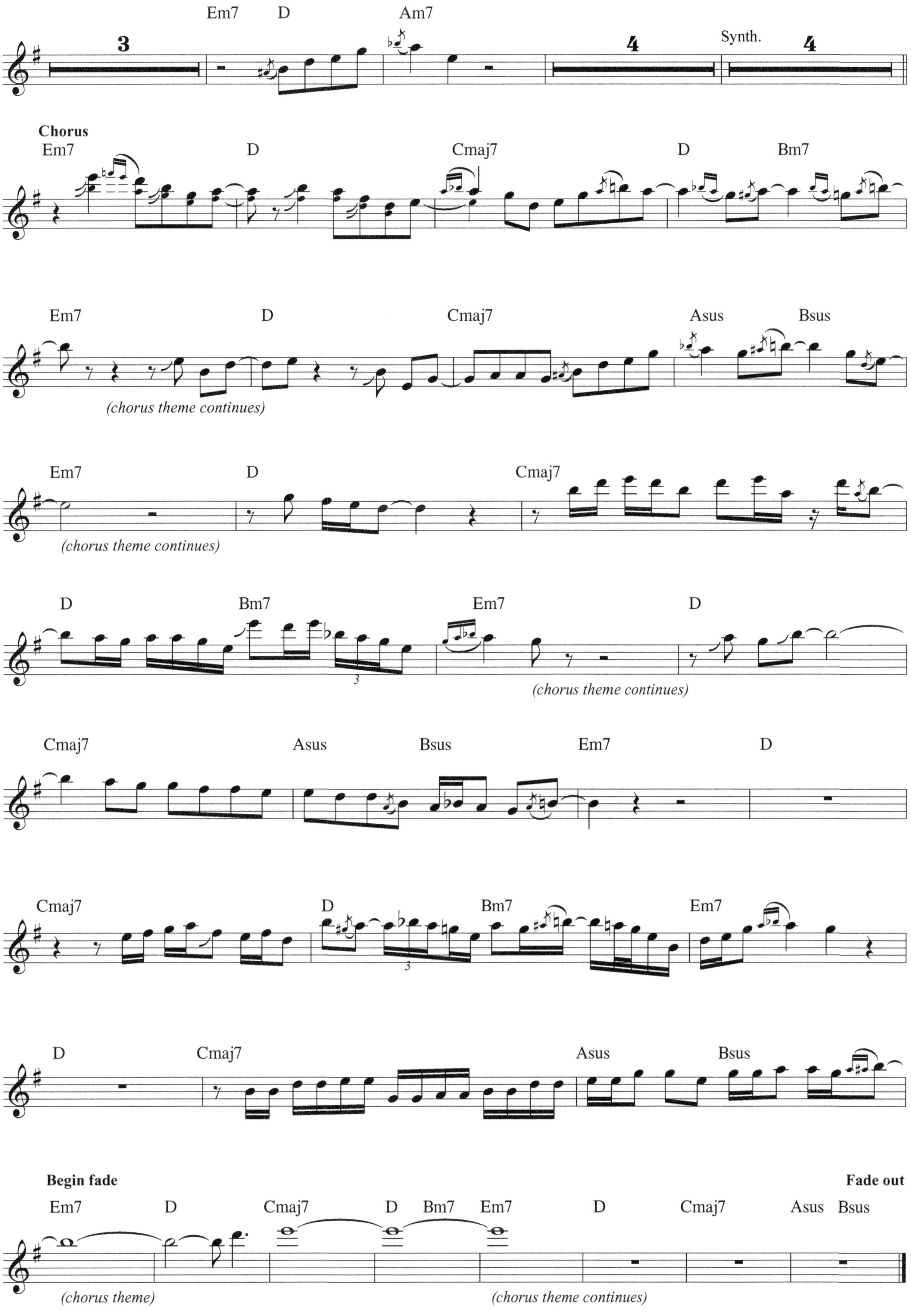
Em7 D Am7
3
4
Synth.
4
Chorus
Em7 D Cmaj7 D Bm7
Em7 D Cmaj7 Asus Bsus
(chorus theme continues)
Em7 D Cmaj7
(chorus theme continues)
D Bm7 Em7 D
(chorus theme continues)
Cmaj7 Asus Bsus Em7 D
Cmaj7 D Bm7 Em7
D Cmaj7 Asus Bsus
Begin fade
Fade out
Em7 D Cmaj7 D Bm7 Em7 D Cmaj7 Asus Bsus
(chorus theme)
(chorus theme continues)

Europa

By Carlos Santana and Tom Coster

Moderately slow (♩ = 66)

Begin fade

Fade out

Flirt

Composed by Mindi Abair and Matthew Hager

Play 3 times

Love Is on the Way

By Dave Koz and Jeff Lorber

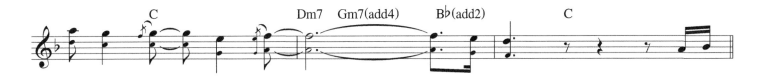

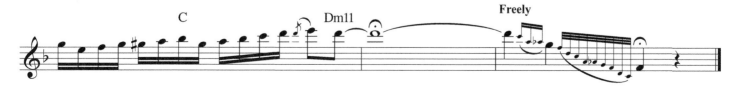

Maputo

By Marcus Miller

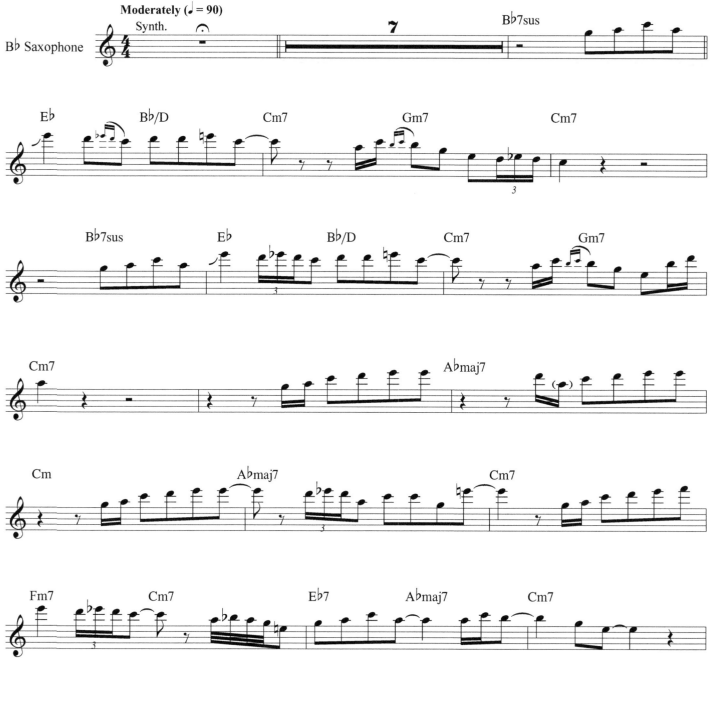

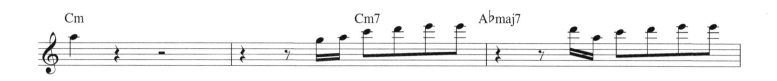

Songbird

By Kenny G

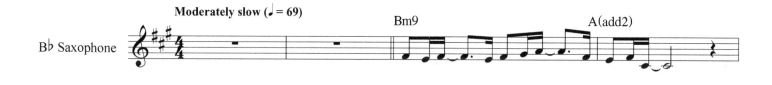

Winelight

Words and Music by William Eaton

Ddim7/C   B♭maj7/C

A7sus   A7   A7sus   A7

A7sus   Dm7

mp

Gm7   Dm7

B♭m7   **To Coda** Dm7

2

mp

Ddim7/C   B♭maj7/C

CODA

Bermuda Nights

By Gerald Albright

Moderately (♩ = 86)

Eb Saxophone

Cm9 C#m9   Dm9   G13   Dm9

                                        C#7#9   F#7b9(b13)

Bm9 C#m7 Dmaj9   8va

Bm9 C#m7 Dmaj9 F#9sus   Bm9   C#m7 Dmaj9

                              Bm9 C#m7 Dmaj9   E13sus   F#9sus

        3   Bm9

        F#7b9(b13)   Bm9   F#7b9(b13)

Bm9   F#7b9(b13)

Bm9   Cm9   C#m9

Blue Water

By Brian Culbertson and Eric Marienthal

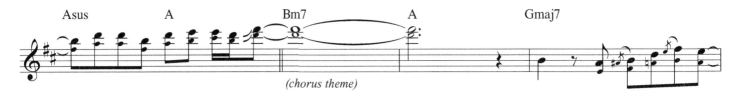

(chorus theme)

(chorus theme continues)

(chorus theme continues)

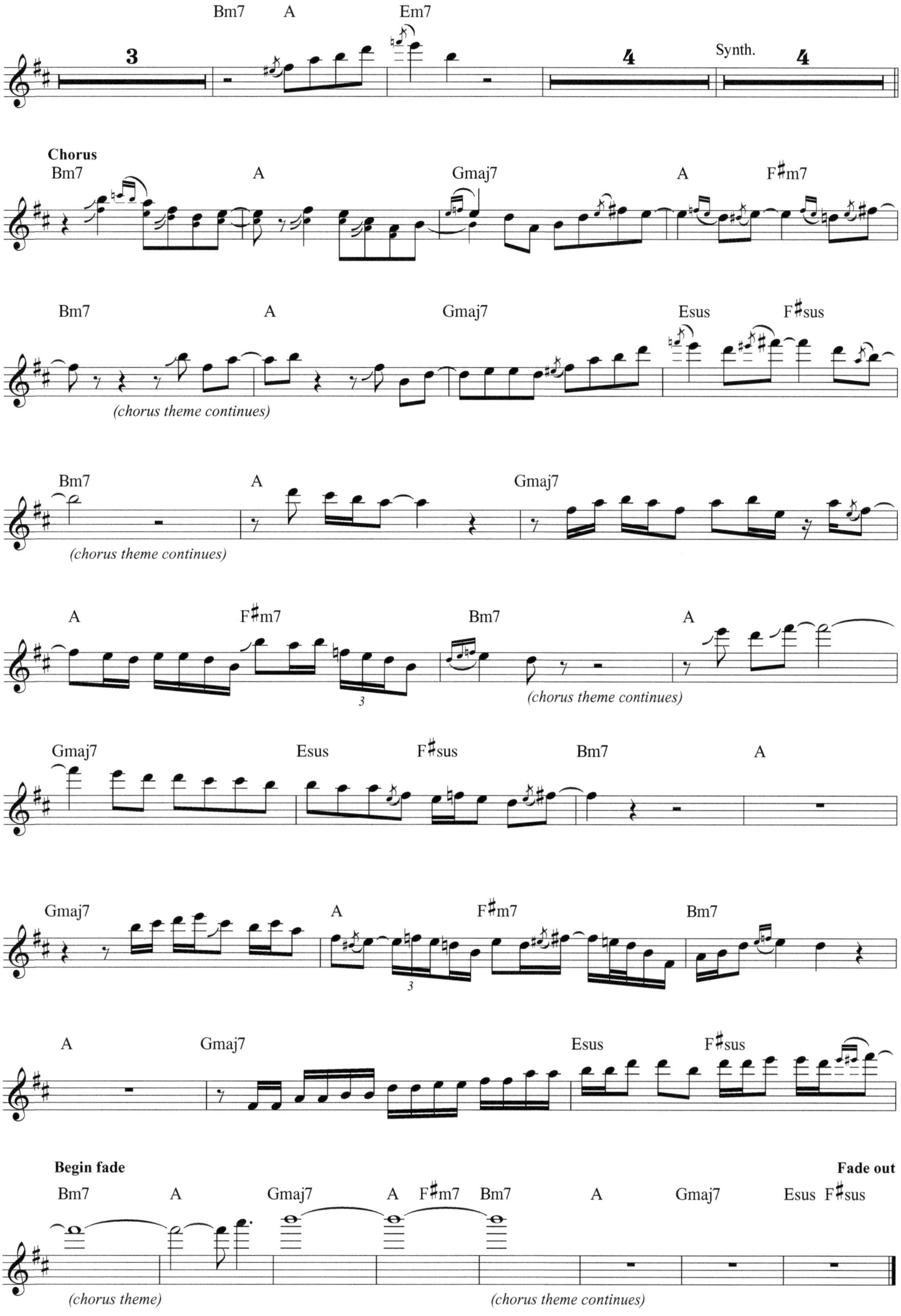
Bm7 A Em7
3
4
Synth. 4
Chorus
Bm7 A Gmaj7 A F♯m7
Bm7 A Gmaj7 Esus F♯sus
(chorus theme continues)
Bm7 A Gmaj7
(chorus theme continues)
A F♯m7 Bm7 A
3
(chorus theme continues)
Gmaj7 Esus F♯sus Bm7 A
Gmaj7 A F♯m7 Bm7
3
A Gmaj7 Esus F♯sus
Begin fade
Fade out
Bm7 A Gmaj7 A F♯m7 Bm7 A Gmaj7 Esus F♯sus
(chorus theme)
(chorus theme continues)

Europa

By Carlos Santana and Tom Coster

Moderately slow ($\quarternote$ = 66)

Eb Saxophone

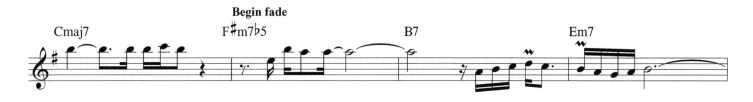

Flirt

Composed by Mindi Abair and Matthew Hager

Play 3 times

Love Is on the Way

By Dave Koz and Jeff Lorber

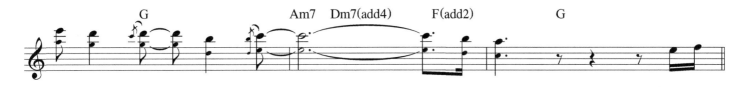

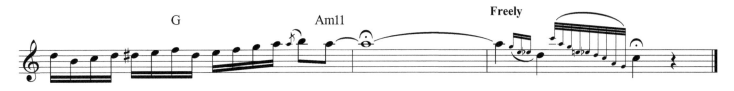

Maputo

By Marcus Miller

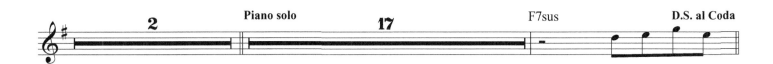

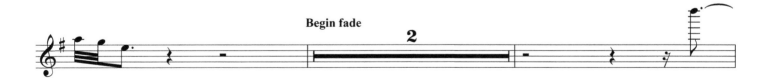

Songbird

By Kenny G

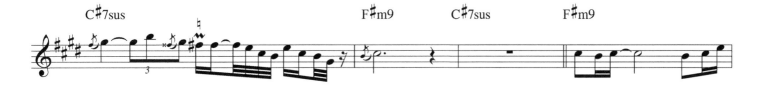

Winelight

Words and Music by William Eaton

CODA

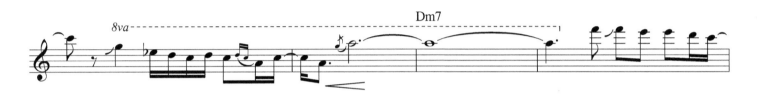

HAL•LEONARD® SAXOPHONE PLAY-ALONG

The Saxophone Play-Along Series will help you play your favorite songs quickly and easily. Just follow the music, listen to the audio to hear how the saxophone should sound, and then play along using the separate backing tracks. Each song is printed twice in the book: once for alto and once for tenor saxes. The online audio is available for streaming or download using the unique code printed inside the book, and it includes **PLAYBACK+** *options such as looping and tempo adjustments.*

1. ROCK 'N' ROLL
Bony Moronie • Charlie Brown • Hand Clappin' • Honky Tonk (Parts 1 & 2) • I'm Walkin' • Lucille (You Won't Do Your Daddy's Will) • See You Later, Alligator • Shake, Rattle and Roll.
00113137 Book/Online Audio $16.99

2. R&B
Cleo's Mood • I Got a Woman • Pick up the Pieces • Respect • Shot Gun • Soul Finger • Soul Serenade • Unchain My Heart.
00113177 Book/Online Audio $16.99

3. CLASSIC ROCK
Baker Street • Deacon Blues • The Heart of Rock and Roll • Jazzman • Smooth Operator • Turn the Page • Who Can It Be Now? • Young Americans.
00113429 Book/Online Audio $16.99

4. SAX CLASSICS
Boulevard of Broken Dreams • Harlem Nocturne • Night Train • Peter Gunn • The Pink Panther • St. Thomas • Tequila • Yakety Sax.
00114393 Book/Online Audio. $16.99

5. CHARLIE PARKER
Billie's Bounce (Bill's Bounce) • Confirmation • Dewey Square • Donna Lee • Now's the Time • Ornithology • Scrapple from the Apple • Yardbird Suite.
00118286 Book/Online Audio $16.99

6. DAVE KOZ
All I See Is You • Can't Let You Go (The Sha La Song) • Emily • Honey-Dipped • Know You by Heart • Put the Top Down • Together Again • You Make Me Smile.
00118292 Book/Online Audio $16.99

7. GROVER WASHINGTON, JR.
East River Drive • Just the Two of Us • Let It Flow • Make Me a Memory (Sad Samba) • Mr. Magic • Take Five • Take Me There • Winelight.
00118293 Book/Online Audio $16.99

8. DAVID SANBORN
Anything You Want • Bang Bang • Chicago Song • Comin' Home Baby • The Dream • Hideaway • Slam • Straight to the Heart.
00125694 Book/Online Audio $16.99

9. CHRISTMAS
The Christmas Song (Chestnuts Roasting on an Open Fire) • Christmas Time Is Here • Count Your Blessings Instead of Sheep • Do You Hear What I Hear • Have Yourself a Merry Little Christmas • The Little Drummer Boy • White Christmas • Winter Wonderland.
00148170 Book/Online Audio $16.99

10. JOHN COLTRANE
Blue Train (Blue Trane) • Body and Soul • Central Park West • Cousin Mary • Giant Steps • Like Sonny (Simple Like) • My Favorite Things • Naima (Niema).
00193333 Book/Online Audio $16.99

11. JAZZ ICONS
Body and Soul • Con Alma • Oleo • Speak No Evil • Take Five • There Will Never Be Another You • Tune Up • Work Song.
00199296 Book/Online Audio $16.99

12. SMOOTH JAZZ
Bermuda Nights • Blue Water • Europa • Flirt • Love Is on the Way • Maputo • Songbird • Winelight.
00248670 Book/Online Audio $16.99

13. BONEY JAMES
Butter • Let It Go • Stone Groove • Stop, Look, Listen (To Your Heart) • Sweet Thing • Tick Tock • Total Experience • Vinyl.
00257186 Book/Online Audio $16.99

IMPROVE YOUR TECHNIQUE

AMAZING PHRASING
50 WAYS TO IMPROVE YOUR IMPROVISATIONAL SKILLS
by Dennis Taylor

Amazing Phrasing is for any sax player interested in learning how to improvise and how to improve their creative phrasing. The ideas are divided into three sections: harmony, rhythm, and melody. The companion audio includes full-band tracks in various musical styles for listening and play along.
00311108 Alto Sax, Book/Online Audio........$19.99
00310787 Tenor Sax, Book/Online Audio......$19.99

PAUL DESMOND
A STEP-BY-STEP BREAKDOWN OF THE SAX STYLES AND TECHNIQUES OF A JAZZ GREAT
by Eric J. Morones

Examine the sophisticated sounds of a jazz sax legend with this instructional pack that explores 12 Desmond classics: Alone Together • Any Other Time • Bossa Antigua • I've Got You Under My Skin • Jazzabelle • Take Five • Take Ten • Time After Time • and more.
00695983 Book/Online Audio $24.99

JAZZ SAXOPHONE
AN IN-DEPTH LOOK AT THE STYLES OF THE TENOR MASTERS
by Dennis Taylor

All the best are here: from the cool bebop excursions of Dexter Gordon, to the stellar musings of John Coltrane, with more than a dozen master players examined in between. Includes lessons, music, historical analysis and rare photos, plus a CD with 16 full-band tracks!
00310983 Book/CD Pack $18.95

MODERN SAXOPHONE TECHNIQUES
by Frank Catalano

Many books present facts, but this guide teaches the developing player how to learn. Listening, exploring, writing original music, and trial and error are some of the methods threaded throughout. On the online video, author and virtuoso saxophonist Frank Catalano offers quick tips on many of the topics covered in the book. Topics include: developing good rhythm • air stream and embouchure • fingering charts • tonguing techniques • modern harmony tips • and more.
00123829 Book/Online Video.......................$24.99

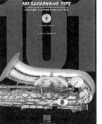

101 SAXOPHONE TIPS
by Eric Morones

This book presents valuable how-to insight that saxophone players of all styles and levels can benefit from. The text, photos, music, diagrams, and accompanying CD provide a terrific, easy-to-use resource for a variety of topics, including: techniques; maintenance; equipment; practicing; recording; performance; and much more!
00311082 Book/CD Pack $19.99

SONNY ROLLINS
A STEP-BY-STEP BREAKDOWN OF THE SAX STYLES & TECHNIQUES OF A JAZZ GIANT

Explore the unique sound and soul of jazz innovator Sonny Rollins on licks from 12 classic songs: Airegin • Biji • Don't Stop the Carnival • Doxy • Duke of Iron • God Bless' the Child • Oleo • St. Thomas • Sonnymoon for Two • Tenor Madness • Way Out West • You Don't Know What Love Is.
00695854 Book/CD Pack $22.99

SAXOPHONE AEROBICS
by Woody Mankowski

This 52-week, one-exercise-a-day workout program for developing, improving and maintaining saxophone technique includes access to demo audio tracks online for all 365 workout licks! Techniques covered include: scales • articulations • rhythms • range extension • arpeggios • ornaments • and stylings. Benefits of using this book include: facile technique • better intonation • increased style vocabulary • heightened rhythmic acuity • improved ensemble playing • and expanded range.
00143344 Book/Online Audio $19.99

THE SAXOPHONE HANDBOOK
COMPLETE GUIDE TO TONE, TECHNIQUE, AND PERFORMANCE
by Douglas D. Skinner
Berklee Press

A complete guide to playing and maintenance, this handbook offers essential information on all dimensions of the saxophone. It provides an overview of technique, such as breathing, fingerings, articulations, and more. Exercises will help you develop your sense of timing, facility, and sound. You'll learn to fine-tune your reed, recork the keys, fix binding keys, replace pads, and many other repairs and adjustments. You'll also learn to improve your tone, intonation, and flexibility while playing with proper technique.
50449658 ....$14.99

SAXOPHONE SOUND EFFECTS
by Ueli Dörig
Berklee Press

Add unique saxophone sounds to your palette of colors! The saxophone is capable of a great range of sounds, from laughs and growls to multiphonics and percussion effects. This book shows you how to do 19 different inventive effects, with etudes that put them in a musical context. The accompanying online audio provides play-along tracks for the etudes and examples of each sound effect in isolation.
50449628 Book/Online Audio $15.99

SAXOPHONE WORKOUT
by Eric J. Morones

This book will give you a complete saxophone workout. Here you'll find etudes that cover a wide spectrum of techniques, from the basics to intermeidate level to advanced. With daily practice that includes use of a metronome and tuner, this book will provide noticeable improvement in the mastery of your horn. The excercises are designed for the trouble spots of all the instruments of the saxophone family – soprano, alto, tenor, baritone – and can be used by players at all levels.
00121478 ....$12.99

25 GREAT SAX SOLOS
TRANSCRIPTIONS • LESSONS • BIOS • PHOTOS
by Eric J. Morones

From Chuck Rio and King Curtis to David Sanborn and Kenny G, take an inside look at the genesis of pop saxophone. This book with online audio provides solo transcriptions in standard notation, lessons on how to play them, bios, equipment, photos, history, and much more. The audio contains full-band demos of every sax solo in the book, and includes the PLAYBACK+ audio player which allows you to adjust the recording to any tempo without changing pitch, loop challenging parts, pan, and more! Songs include: After the Love Has Gone • Deacon Blues • Just the Two of Us • Just the Way You Are • Mercy, Mercy Me • Money • Respect • Spooky • Take Five • Tequila • Yakety Sax • and more.
00311315 Book/Online Audio $22.99

HAL•LEONARD®
www.halleonard.com

Prices, content, and availability subject to change without notice.

HAL•LEONARD INSTRUMENTAL PLAY-ALONG

Your favorite songs are arranged just for solo instrumentalists with this outstanding series. Each book includes great full-accompaniment play-along audio so you can sound just like a pro!

Check out **halleonard.com** for songlists and more titles!

12 Pop Hits
12 songs
00261790	Flute	00261795	Horn
00261791	Clarinet	00261796	Trombone
00261792	Alto Sax	00261797	Violin
00261793	Tenor Sax	00261798	Viola
00261794	Trumpet	00261799	Cello

The Very Best of Bach
15 selections
00225371	Flute	00225376	Horn
00225372	Clarinet	00225377	Trombone
00225373	Alto Sax	00225378	Violin
00225374	Tenor Sax	00225379	Viola
00225375	Trumpet	00225380	Cello

The Beatles
15 songs
00225330	Flute	00225335	Horn
00225331	Clarinet	00225336	Trombone
00225332	Alto Sax	00225337	Violin
00225333	Tenor Sax	00225338	Viola
00225334	Trumpet	00225339	Cello

Chart Hits
12 songs
00146207	Flute	00146212	Horn
00146208	Clarinet	00146213	Trombone
00146209	Alto Sax	00146214	Violin
00146210	Tenor Sax	00146211	Trumpet
00146216	Cello		

Christmas Songs
12 songs
00146855	Flute	00146863	Horn
00146858	Clarinet	00146864	Trombone
00146859	Alto Sax	00146866	Violin
00146860	Tenor Sax	00146867	Viola
00146862	Trumpet	00146868	Cello

Contemporary Broadway
15 songs
00298704	Flute	00298709	Horn
00298705	Clarinet	00298710	Trombone
00298706	Alto Sax	00298711	Violin
00298707	Tenor Sax	00298712	Viola
00298708	Trumpet	00298713	Cello

Disney Movie Hits
12 songs
00841420	Flute	00841424	Horn
00841687	Oboe	00841425	Trombone
00841421	Clarinet	00841426	Violin
00841422	Alto Sax	00841427	Viola
00841686	Tenor Sax	00841428	Cello
00841423	Trumpet		

Prices, contents, and availability subject to change without notice.

Disney characters and artwork ™ & © 2021 Disney

Disney Solos
12 songs
00841404	Flute	00841506	Oboe
00841406	Alto Sax	00841409	Trumpet
00841407	Horn	00841410	Violin
00841411	Viola	00841412	Cello
00841405	Clarinet/Tenor Sax		
00841408	Trombone/Baritone		
00841553	Mallet Percussion		

Dixieland Favorites
15 songs
00268756	Flute	0068759	Trumpet
00268757	Clarinet	00268760	Trombone
00268758	Alto Sax		

Billie Eilish
9 songs
00345648	Flute	00345653	Horn
00345649	Clarinet	00345654	Trombone
00345650	Alto Sax	00345655	Violin
00345651	Tenor Sax	00345656	Viola
00345652	Trumpet	00345657	Cello

Favorite Movie Themes
13 songs
00841166	Flute	00841168	Trumpet
00841167	Clarinet	00841170	Trombone
00841169	Alto Sax	00841296	Violin

Gospel Hymns
15 songs
00194648	Flute	00194654	Trombone
00194649	Clarinet	00194655	Violin
00194650	Alto Sax	00194656	Viola
00194651	Tenor Sax	00194657	Cello
00194652	Trumpet		

Great Classical Themes
15 songs
00292727	Flute	00292733	Horn
00292728	Clarinet	00292735	Trombone
00292729	Alto Sax	00292736	Violin
00292730	Tenor Sax	00292737	Viola
00292732	Trumpet	00292738	Cello

The Greatest Showman
8 songs
00277389	Flute	00277394	Horn
00277390	Clarinet	00277395	Trombone
00277391	Alto Sax	00277396	Violin
00277392	Tenor Sax	00277397	Viola
00277393	Trumpet	00277398	Cello

Irish Favorites
31 songs
00842489	Flute	00842495	Trombone
00842490	Clarinet	00842496	Violin
00842491	Alto Sax	00842497	Viola
00842493	Trumpet	00842498	Cello
00842494	Horn		

Michael Jackson
11 songs
00119495	Flute	00119499	Trumpet
00119496	Clarinet	00119501	Trombone
00119497	Alto Sax	00119503	Violin
00119498	Tenor Sax	00119502	Accomp.

Jazz & Blues
14 songs
00841438	Flute	00841441	Trumpet
00841439	Clarinet	00841443	Trombone
00841440	Alto Sax	00841444	Violin
00841442	Tenor Sax		

Jazz Classics
12 songs
00151812	Flute	00151816	Trumpet
00151813	Clarinet	00151818	Trombone
00151814	Alto Sax	00151819	Violin
00151815	Tenor Sax	00151821	Cello

Les Misérables
13 songs
00842292	Flute	00842297	Horn
00842293	Clarinet	00842298	Trombone
00842294	Alto Sax	00842299	Violin
00842295	Tenor Sax	00842300	Viola
00842296	Trumpet	00842301	Cello

Metallica
12 songs
02501327	Flute	02502454	Horn
02501339	Clarinet	02501329	Trombone
02501332	Alto Sax	02501334	Violin
02501333	Tenor Sax	02501335	Viola
02501330	Trumpet	02501338	Cello

Motown Classics
15 songs
00842572	Flute	00842576	Trumpet
00842573	Clarinet	00842578	Trombone
00842574	Alto Sax	00842579	Violin
00842575	Tenor Sax		

Pirates of the Caribbean
16 songs
00842183	Flute	00842188	Horn
00842184	Clarinet	00842189	Trombone
00842185	Alto Sax	00842190	Violin
00842186	Tenor Sax	00842191	Viola
00842187	Trumpet	00842192	Cello

Queen
17 songs
00285402	Flute	00285407	Horn
00285403	Clarinet	00285408	Trombone
00285404	Alto Sax	00285409	Violin
00285405	Tenor Sax	00285410	Viola
00285406	Trumpet	00285411	Cello

Simple Songs
14 songs
00249081	Flute	00249087	Horn
00249093	Oboe	00249089	Trombone
00249082	Clarinet	00249090	Violin
00249083	Alto Sax	00249091	Viola
00249084	Tenor Sax	00249092	Cello
00249086	Trumpet	00249094	Mallets

Superhero Themes
14 songs
00363195	Flute	00363200	Horn
00363196	Clarinet	00363201	Trombone
00363197	Alto Sax	00363202	Violin
00363198	Tenor Sax	00363203	Viola
00363199	Trumpet	00363204	Cello

Star Wars
16 songs
00350900	Flute	00350907	Horn
00350913	Oboe	00350908	Trombone
00350903	Clarinet	00350909	Violin
00350904	Alto Sax	00350910	Viola
00350905	Tenor Sax	00350911	Cello
00350906	Trumpet	00350914	Mallet

Taylor Swift
15 songs
00842532	Flute	00842537	Horn
00842533	Clarinet	00842538	Trombone
00842534	Alto Sax	00842539	Violin
00842535	Tenor Sax	00842540	Viola
00842536	Trumpet	00842541	Cello

Video Game Music
13 songs
00283877	Flute	00283883	Horn
00283878	Clarinet	00283884	Trombone
00283879	Alto Sax	00283885	Violin
00283880	Tenor Sax	00283886	Viola
00283882	Trumpet	00283887	Cello

Wicked
13 songs
00842236	Flute	00842241	Horn
00842237	Clarinet	00842242	Trombone
00842238	Alto Sax	00842243	Violin
00842239	Tenor Sax	00842244	Viola
00842240	Trumpet	00842245	Cello

HAL•LEONARD®